What Filled the Spot?

Written by Lisa Thompson
Pictures by Craig Smith

The sea star munched on the seaweed.

"Yum! That filled the spot," said the sea star.

3

The little fish munched on the sea star.

"Yum! That filled the spot," said
the little fish.

The big fish munched on the little fish.

"Yum! That filled the spot," said
the big fish.

The shark munched on the big fish.

"I'm still hungry," said the shark. He saw another big fish and munched on that too.

"Ouch!" cried the shark.

A hook was stuck in his teeth.

The shark was angry.

10

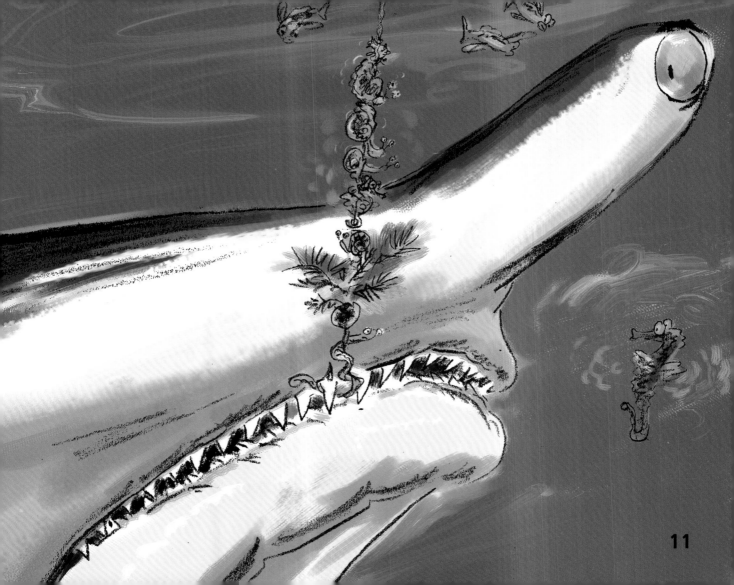

11

"I think I've got something,"
said the Captain.

"You've got me!" said the shark,
snapping his teeth.

"And you'd better watch out.
I'm still hungry!"

16